Anger Management

The Complete Psychologist's Guide to Recognizing and Controlling Anger – Develop Emotional Self-Awareness and Eliminate Anxiety, Stress and Depression

Brandon Cooper

Table of Contents

Introduction: Anger & Your Brain

Congratulations on getting a copy of *Anger Management: The Complete Psychologist's Guide to Recognizing and Controlling Anger – Develop Emotional Self-Awareness and Eliminate Anxiety, Stress and Depression*. This book will help you identify what is causing your anger, and will help you learn to control your emotions and live a happier, healthier life free from the anger's hold.

In this introduction, you will learn about how anger affects your brain. Anger is a lot more than 'just another emotion,' and it is important to understand what happens to both your brain and body when you experience anger. Recognizing these physiological changes can help you identify anger in its early stages and also help you manage all facets of your anger better.

So, what is anger? By definition, anger is an emotional state that can vary in intensity from mild irritation to full-blown rage. When you experience anger, you also experience biological or physiological changes. For example, your blood pressure goes up and your heart rate increases, and you also experience increased levels in your adrenaline, noradrenaline, and energy hormones.

Anger can have a variety of causes, but is typically related to either an internal or external event. These events could include a simple traffic jam, a memory of a traumatic event, or a conflict with a friend or coworker.

Our instinct is to react to anger with aggression. This is part of our "fight or flight" response. Typically, the root of our anger is

"

connected to some type of perceived threat, and anger is actually necessary for our survival.

But life cannot be lived in a constant state of anger, so it is important to understand how to manage your anger and create a healthier life for yourself as a result.

There are three approaches to anger: expressing, suppressing and calming. Expressing your anger can be healthy, as long as it is done in an assertive as opposed to an aggressive manner. The difference between being *assertive* and being *aggressive* is respect; when you are assertive, you are still respectful of others, as well as yourself, whereas aggression shows respect for no one.

Suppressing your anger is not the healthiest choice, but it can be effective at times. The point of suppression would be to inhibit the anger and then converting it into something more constructive. Unfortunately, this method can be self-destructive and can lead to permanent issues like high blood pressure, depression, or hypertension. Suppressing your anger can also lead to passive-aggressive behavior, or becoming cynical or hostile towards others. A negative attitude will have a negative effect on your relationships, both personal and professional. Because of this, it may be in your best interest to express your anger rather than suppress it.

Finally, calming yourself can be an effective way to handle your anger. If you can regain control by practicing breathing exercises or even meditating, you will lower your heart rate and also lower your blood pressure. By calming yourself down and stopping the physiological reactions to anger, you will find it much easier to manage the emotional reactions to anger as well.

Remember: the goal of anger management is not to stop yourself from feeling anger, but to reduce your reactions to anger, both emotional and physical. This is especially important because you will never be able to control others; all you can control is your own reaction to the actions of others.

Throughout your life, your subconscious will record in memory everything you say, everything you do, and even everything you think. Meanwhile, your conscious mind controls how you respond to people in any given moment, giving it a lot more influence over your emotional state. While your subconscious has little to do with your emotions, it does record the patterns of how you respond to certain things or people, and it trains your body to respond to those things in the same way each time.

For example, your subconscious contains what most people call 'muscle memory.' That means your subconscious will learn how you respond to a stimulating event, and it will recreate in your muscles that same response each and every time the stimulating event occurs, just like how your hands seem to always remember where the keys on the keyboard are. This 'muscle memory' allows you to respond very quickly to situations you've been conditioned for, which is a necessary part of survival. A slow response, or even a lack of response, can put your life at risk, and it is the responsibility of your subconscious to tell your consciousness how to react in order to protect you.

This is often referred to as a 'fight or flight' response. Your brain tells your body how to react, so that in a threatening or potentially deadly situation, your body can react immediately for the sake of self-preservation. You could even consider this as a 'safety feature' built into your body.

This response is innate. Our ancestors needed the 'fight or flight' response to survive. They did not have time to stop and think about how they should respond to a vicious predator hunting them down. They had to react immediately and without doubt if they wanted to live.

Over time, our brains have taken this kind of response to a whole new level. People experience immediate reactions to certain triggering events, and those triggers are different for everyone.

Is this beyond my control? Can I retrain my subconscious to respond differently?

The good news is that it is not beyond your control, and you absolutely can retrain your subconscious to respond differently. It will not be easy, but with the help of the information in this book you will be successful in teaching your brain how to respond to triggering stimuli properly.

Ultimately, your anger is your own fault. That might be hard to hear and maybe harder yet to accept. But how you respond to life is a decision only you can make, and if you choose to respond with anger, then it is simply your fault. Once you can acknowledge and accept that, you can begin to investigate why you first responded with anger. Figuring out why you responded the way you did will help you change the way you deal with various situations, and will help you prevent your anger from having too much of an effect on your life.

So, what are triggers? What makes you angry? Keeping a 'frustration journal' has been proven to be beneficial for people who get angry easily. Each time a person gets angry, he or she can write about what made him or her feel angry, and why.

Once they have returned to a calm and rational state of mind, the person can re-read what they wrote, and start creating solutions for their anger issues.

These are the most common triggers for anger:

- When one feels everyone in his/her surroundings thinks he/she is stupid
- When one feels disrespected
- When one feels ignored and invisible

Now, your triggers may be different, but these are the most commonly reported. A person may have more triggers than another, or in contrast, a person may have only one trigger for their anger. This book will help you know, understand, and address each trigger that you have. Some might be so specific and hide so well within other triggers that it will take months of introspection for you to identify them.

When a trigger occurs, you may not even notice it right away, but your brain will. Different parts of your consciousness will acknowledge the trigger and start sending signals throughout your brain. Eventually, the signal will make its way to your pituitary and adrenal glands. These parts are where your body's hormones are stored. Most of the time, a trigger will cause your brain to start overproducing hormones like cortisol and adrenaline.

An overload of these hormones can lead to a variety of physical reactions. Your heart rate may increase, your blood pressure may spike, and you may experience a sudden migraine or a headache. Too much cortisol or adrenaline over time may even lead to serious health concerns, like an increased risk of cancer, heart attacks, and strokes.

These health concerns are exactly why it is so important for you to learn how to take control of your anger now while you still can. Is your anger worth risking your life and your health? The answer is obviously no.

So, let us retrain your brain to respond differently to whatever it is that made you so angry before! This book aims to help you learn how to live a healthier, happier, and a less-angry life.

Chapter 1: The Root of Your Anger

It is now time to identify your triggers. Grab a notebook or journal, and start writing in it each time you get upset about something. Do your very best to spill every emotion onto the page and not into your life. Write down what happened, how it made you feel, and then start to think about why it made you feel that way. Did something similar happen to you as a child? Be specific and write as much as you need to. In fact, do not stop writing until your heartbeat has settled and your respirations have returned to a normal and steady rate.

Try not to cast blame. While you are writing, avoid pointing the finger at one particular person. After all, it is not the person that made you angry but something that they said or did. Most of the time, the people who make you angry are not trying to make you angry, and it is incredibly important for you to recognize that it may have been accidental on their part. Assuming the worst and allowing your anger to color your opinion of that person or your view of your relationship with that person will only serve to make things worse.

Next time you feel yourself getting angry, take a deep breath and step away from the situation. Not sure how to excuse yourself from a tense situation? Try one of these simple, respectful phrases:

- "I don't think this is the right time to discuss this."
- "I need some time to think before we discuss this."
- "We should revisit this at a later date."
- "Can we talk about this later?"
- "I need a few minutes, please."

Remember to always respond with respect, no matter how angry you may feel. Responding disrespectfully will only allow the situation to escalate, which will only make you angrier and make it harder for you to control your emotions.

One psychologist who specializes in anger management, Jeffrey Deffenbacher, Ph.D., explains that some people are simply more "hotheaded" than other people. They often find themselves reaching a point of anger very quickly compared to others, and they tend to feel that anger more intensely and for a longer period of time.

It is important to remember that anger may be displayed differently from person to person. Some people may be prone to yelling, cursing, or throwing things, while others may just be chronically grumpy, easily irritated, socially withdrawn, or even physically ill. Anger is not always loud.

Those who frequently experience bouts of anger also tend to have a lower tolerance for inconvenience or irritation. Sometimes, the predisposition for anger is genetic. Sometimes, it is sociocultural or environmental. Individuals raised in a home with an angry parent are more likely to become angry person themselves. The more chaotic or disruptive your household is, the more likely you are to experience anger and struggle with managing that anger.

Very few people are taught how to express anger as children. In fact, children are often punished for expressing their anger. Many psychologists are now encouraging parents to let their children cycle through the various emotions that they experience when they get angry. Allowing your children to have a "temper tantrum," and then having an open and honest discussion about what made them feel that way, and how they can stop themselves from feeling out of control or overwhelmed, may be incredibly beneficial later in life.

Anger is not something to be ashamed of, as long as you are able to control it and prevent it from taking over your life, your health, and your well-being.

The person to blame for your anger will always be you, though it is not always easy to accept that blame. But ultimately, deciding how to respond is a choice that you will make. You need to retrain your brain to respond differently from how it usually does, because you now understand that your emotions are your responsibility. Anger is your fault just as joy is your fault. You get to choose how you respond to the good and bad moments in life. It is completely within your control.

Why let someone else ruin your day? If you allow someone or something else to control your emotions, you are giving that person entirely too much power over your life, your emotions, and your well-being. You are giving them entirely too much control.

Instead, take control of your own life and your own emotions. You can start this journey by identifying your triggers. Are there certain words that upset you? For many people, silly taunts from their childhood have lasting effects, and they may find themselves feeling irrationally angry when they hear one person call another person names meant to insult their intelligence, class, race, gender, or sexual orientation.

Are there certain actions that upset you? A person can get incredibly angry every time someone lies to him or her. While it is easy to understand why a lie would upset someone so much, it's also very vital to find a way to understand that lies are not a reflection of the person who was lied to. Lies are only a reflection of the person who chose to lie. So, why get angry over it? Lies are a symptom of low self-worth, and what good will anger do when the person lying to you already has such a low opinion of themselves?

Once you have identified some of your triggers, it is important to explore why they exist as triggers for you. Our emotions are rooted in our childhood and adolescence. How we respond to what happens in our life is shaped almost entirely by the way we were raised and the way people around us responded. If we need to change the way we respond to something, we need to first understand how we learned to respond as we do.

Feeling as though you lack control over yourself or the situation you are in is the primary reason for anger. Are there things in your life that make you feel as if you don't have any control over them?

Another thing that can trigger an angry response is the feeling of irresponsibility. If a person makes an irresponsible choice, it can eat them up until they blow up with anger. The person may feel that they are burdened by his responsibilities because they are a large part of their life. The person may also feel that the poor choices they have made negatively reflect what kind of a person they are.

It can be very difficult to let go of anger when the root of the anger is fear. Some people are afraid that the actions or choices of others would reflect poorly on them, that their reputation would be negatively affected, or that if others would think less of them as a result of the decisions that other people made.

However, that idea is completely ridiculous! Your life is your life. No one is responsible for your life other than you. You make your own choices. You control your own life. The actions of others do not reflect on you because you are your own person.

If you allow someone to control your emotions and make you respond with anger, then you're allowing that person to control your life as well as your emotions. Why would you allow that? Take control! Accept responsibility for every feeling that you have, positive or negative, and start working hard to discover what or who is making you feel very angry. Your life and decisions are yours, not theirs.

Dig deep. If you cannot identify on your own what triggers you and why, consider reaching out to a counselor or therapist that specializes in anger management. They may provide the outside perspective and voice of reason you need to truly understand yourself and your reactions. Emotions are rarely easy to understand, especially if you are not an inherently intuitive person.

Anger is always presented as a negative emotion, but it is neither good nor bad. You should not be embarrassed or ashamed by the emotion. You should not try to live your life without ever experiencing anger. Understand that anger happens to the best of us.

Anger, like any emotion, is meant to convey a message between your brain and your body. It is often a knee-jerk reaction based on some sort of fear, and because of the rush of adrenaline that floods your body when you get angry, it is hard to recognize what is making you angry, or why it is making you angry. The key is not to AVOID anger, but to express it in a healthy, respectful way.

Is it healthy to vent, and let your anger out? While it is not healthy to suppress or hide your anger, it is also not healthy to vent too much. You should find a balance where you do not need to express your anger in an aggressive way. Tirades and outbursts only make the situation worse.

Will expressing your anger earn you respect? If you cannot express your anger in a healthy way, you will only come across a tyrant or a bully. This will not earn your respect. It will only teach others to fear you, to avoid you, and even to lie you to you if they feel you may react negatively to what they have to say.

What if you feel that your anger is something that cannot be controlled? While you cannot control every situation that you find yourself in, and you cannot control how these situations make you feel, you can ALWAYS control how to express yourself. You do not have to express your anger in a verbally or physically abusive way. You can always, always respond with respect and humility.

Most people in your situation think that they are handling their anger in a completely responsible matter and that the people around them are just "too sensitive." This attitude will quickly damage your relationships, prevent you from succeeding in life, impair your judgment, and have an overall negative impact not only on your life but also on the way others see you.

Anger management is not about suppressing your anger or ignoring it. It is not about never allowing yourself to feel anger deeply enough to affect your judgement. The primary goal of anger management is to simply understand why you feel the way you do, and how to express that healthily and respectfully. If you can change the way you express your anger, you will quickly find that your personal and working relationships will become stronger, and your overall quality of life will improve.

Managing your anger takes a serious commitment. It is not be easy, but it will get easier the longer you work at it. This is especially true when you see your work is leading to stronger relationships, goals being achieved, and a healthier and more satisfying life.

If you cannot find a way to manage your anger, you will see it have significant effects on your physical health. High levels of anger and stress will only make you more likely to develop heart disease, insomnia, diabetes, high blood pressure, and a weakened immune system.

Uncontrolled anger also has a significant effect on your mental health. It makes it difficult to concentrate, clouds your thinking, leads to depression and other mental health concerns.

Uncontrolled anger will also hurt your career. Outbursts and episodes of lashing out will only alienate your coworkers, your clients, and your supervisors. You will quickly lose their respect. You have to find a way to channel your anger into constructive criticism and respectful debate in order to be seen as a reliable employee.

Finally, uncontrolled anger will only hurt your personal relationships. It will leave lasting scars on your relationships, and make it difficult for your friends and family to trust you. It will also make it difficult for the people in your life to speak to you honestly or be comfortable around you.

Anger is not only caused by fear, but it also breeds fear. Isn't it time to stop fear from ruling your life, and finally take control over your anger?

Chapter 2: Anger & Your Health

As already mentioned, your brain responds to anger by releasing an excess of cortisol and adrenaline. These same hormones are also triggered by feelings of fear, anxiety, or excitement. The excess cortisol and adrenaline that is released from the adrenal glands flood the body, and the brain immediately sends more blood to your muscles because it assumes you are experiencing a 'fight or flight' situation.

This assumption means that the body is then prepared for some sort of immediate physical action. Your body temperature will start to rise, and you may begin to sweat. Your heart rate will increase, your blood pressure will elevate, and your breathing will change.

These changes are not harmful if they are momentary. But anger is rarely momentary for those who struggle with anger management.

Allowing stress chemicals like cortisol and adrenaline to flood your body regularly can wreak havoc on your body. It will lead to serious metabolic changes, and can cause the following issues:

- An increase in the frequency and severity of headaches
- An increase in the frequency and severity of migraines
- Depression
- Anxiety
- Insomnia
- Irritable bowel syndrome
- Changes in appetite
- Changes in weight

- Acne or eczema
- Increased blood pressure
- Decreased thyroid function
- Heart attack or other heart-related conditions
- Stroke

Studies have even shown that high levels of stress hormones can contribute to your risk factors for cancer.

There are typically two types of reactions to anger for the person experiencing it: explosion and repression. Allowing yourself to experience 'fits of rage' often leads to violent or physically harmful behavior. It also leads to low self-esteem and has a seriously negative effect on interpersonal relationships. Meanwhile, repressing your anger often leads to depression, anxiety, poor communication with others, and the destruction of interpersonal relationships.

Neither reaction is appropriate or healthy, which is why it is so important to learn how to control your emotions enough to choose another reaction. If you can identify what makes you angry, and stop the anger in its tracks, you will never need to worry about the havoc anger can wreak on your life ever again.

In the heat of the moment, often the most healthy reaction you can have is to walk away. Take a few minutes to collect yourself, calm down, and identify the root of your emotions. This is often a good time to meditate or practice mindfulness.

If you are looking for a more long-term solution to outbursts, look for healthy ways to regularly express the anger you may feel through physical activity. Join a gym or organized sport and take boxing lessons, etc.

It is important for you to practice mindfulness every day. Keep a diary that details how you feel, when, and why. Learn to meditate or start taking yoga classes. Exercise regularly. Make sure you have plenty of time to practice 'self-care,' even if that self-care is just a long bath and a good book. And if these little acts of mindfulness are not enough, find a counselor or psychologist in your area. They might be able to provide you with additional help to manage your emotions and stress, or they may provide you with medication that can help you.

Most important though, is for you to remember that stress amplifies anger. If you are stressed about something going on at work or at home, you are much more likely to experience anger because your stress levels are already high, and your body is already full of those dreaded stress hormones.

Many studies have shown that a regular exercise routine can reduce stress levels; it is strongly recommended to use physical activity to safely release the stress hormones that are clogging up the brain's pathways. Exercise releases endorphins, and endorphins will override your stress to put a stop to anger faster than anything else.

Start a routine

What physical activity makes you tick? It doesn't have to be something incredibly strenuous, like running, or something completely engrossing, like freehand rock climbing. If it's badminton, try to join a badminton team. Team sports are one of the best exercises to do for anger management because they help improve your relationships with other people. You experience less anger when you are successfully cooperating with other people. This will also give you a leg up at work in situations where you have to do group projects with others.

If you love swimming, join a gym that has a pool. You may want to try out several different exercises to find one that keeps your interest, which can be a fun process. Eventually, you will find one that you enjoy, and systematically trying out new things, perhaps with friends, can be an adventure and stress-reliever in and of itself.

Trying new exercises is the easy part. It's sticking with your new plan that is most difficult. However, if you are serious about managing your anger, you must incorporate exercise into your life. There are a few ways to ensure you stick with your routine.

First, try to visualize the benefits you are creating in your body. Exercise relieves high blood pressure, decreases your risk of heart attack, and stroke, improves circulation, and most importantly decreases your stress levels. In short, exercise counter-effects some of the worst effects of anger and stress, making it absolutely necessary for anger management; see if it is motivating for you to think about every exercise session as taking a step away from the negative realm of your anger. No matter what, it makes you look and feel better about yourself, an added psychological benefit.

Remember, you don't have to exercise every single day, but it is a good idea to do it 3-5 times a week, for forty-five minutes to an hour each session. Less than this will give you less noticeable benefits.

It may be difficult to visualize yourself going for a run every morning if you've always hated running, or an afternoon swim if you despise the ocean, especially if you normally do not incorporate exercise into your day. That's why when making an important and monumental change like this, you have to ask yourself: What have I enjoyed in the past? What activities were a part of memories I truly enjoyed? You want to pick something you enjoy doing, or you aren't likely to stick with it. You won't always want to get out of bed an hour early or go to the gym after working all day. That's why you have to do exercises that you associate with good feelings: it gives you a little extra motivation.

Exercise not only helps relieve stress, it gives you the satisfaction of taking care of yourself. Everyone knows that exercise is beneficial to your health. It slims you down and tones your body, making you feel better about your physical appearance. Exercise also improves your sleep cycles, which very well may have been previously disrupted by your stress and anger. These things can easily keep you up at night, causing you to lose sleep, sleep less deeply, and become even more stressed out - which in turn causes even more anger in an endless unhealthy cycle. But you can break that cycle!

After an exercise session, you feel calm and relaxed. This, coupled with purposeful breathing exercises, can help you become a more physically relaxed person in general, making it easier to deal with stress.

Besides the physical benefits of exercise, it has mental benefits as well. Exercise releases endorphins into the brain, which cause you to feel happier. It helps relieve stress. It combats depression. All of these things are a huge help when combating anger, but in order to achieve these results through exercise, it takes time and dedication. You must implement your exercise routine and *you must stick with it to see a change.*

Besides implementing a daily routine, exercise is also beneficial when dealing with situational stress. Imagine yourself in a stressful situation: You are at work. Jack from accounting is bugging you for a weekly progress report, which isn't due until tomorrow, and you haven't completed it yet. He said he needs it by today. This causes your stress levels to rise to an uncomfortable level. You begin breathing rapidly, activating your fight-or-flight mode. But you implement your breathing techniques and manage your anger as properly as you can as you return to your desk. Good job!

However, the feeling of stress lingers on. Throughout the day, you can't stop thinking about Jack and his impossible expectations. It makes you mad.

At the end of the day, you leave the office. At this point, you have two options: One, you can bring this anger home with you to your family. You will arrive stressed and irritated, possibly causing you to have an inappropriate angry reaction with your family, or even in traffic on the way home. Option two during your commute home would be doing deep breathing exercises; this should help to dispel your anger quickly, but remember, everyone is different. Don't get discouraged if breathing alone doesn't make you feel like you have immediately solved your problems.

Another option after a day of building anger is to do a quick ten- or fifteen-minute workout. The workout will help to relieve your situational stress and anger just by making you feel physically better. You will focus all your energy, not internally as stress, or externally on your family, but into your own body completing an activity. Your stress will burn itself away, along with all those calories. Endorphins will be released in your brain, making you feel happier and reducing even more of the sensations of stress and anger. It doesn't take long to work up a sweat and help yourself out of a stressful situation! In as little as ten minutes you can find yourself feeling better.

By using quick-workouts as a response to situational stress, you let your body get rid of that stress in the best way possible. You leave the stress behind you on the treadmill and are able to continue home to your family, providing them the kind of stress and anger-free environment that they deserve.

While exercise is one of the best things you can do for excessive stress in your life, there are some very important pitfalls to avoid. You don't want to use exercise as a crutch, instead of having an anger plan or addressing your issues with the people affected by your anger. Reducing anger with exercise only works in tandem with the other steps of anger management.

Although exercise is one of the best ways to help manage your anger, there is one common problem which must be addressed: substituting exercise for violence. That is a dangerous road to walk. Many people with anger issues have strong desires to be violent. For example, you may want to punch Jack in the face for asking for his progress report inconveniently early. *This is not a healthy desire, and it needs to be addressed in order for you move on from your anger.* However, it cannot be addressed with exercise alone.

Feeling a desire to physically hurt someone else is a problem that many people with anger issues face. People think that the best way to avoid hurting someone is by taking the anger out on an inanimate object, perhaps while fantasizing that the object is the person whom they want to hurt. A common example of this is using a punching bag at the gym. You go in and take all your anger, aggression and violent urges out on this punching bag, pretending it is Jack from accounting. *This is not a healthy practice.*

Although this may seem harmless, and many believe it is therapeutic, it is counterproductive to good anger management and good mental health in general. When you act in a violent manner or release aggression through violent actions, you are not addressing the real issues behind the anger. After you abuse an inanimate object, you may feel exhausted, and perhaps your aggressive feelings will be gone, but where did they go? The answer is, nowhere good or productive. These feelings have not been deescalated properly as they are with exercises such as biking, running or team sports, which help balance our mental and emotional state of being.

Although violence toward inanimate objects may feel good at the time and help release tension, it plays a trick on the mind. It trains our bodies to feel stress-relief from physical violence, which is still a loss of self-control. Remember, for proper anger management, violence of any sort is never okay. It is not cathartic or therapeutic, and by maintaining a habit of violent behavior, it hurts us much more than it helps.

Retrain your brain

As already discussed, anger is a learned behavior. You are angry because you have taught yourself to respond to certain stimuli with anger. The only way to combat this is to retrain your brain to respond differently.

You can do this every day in the following ways:

- Treat others as you would want to be treated. If someone makes a mistake, do not immediately respond with anger. Pause and reflect on how you would like to be treated if you made a similar mistake.

- Before you speak, think about how you would feel if someone said to you what you are or were about to say. Is it respectful? Is it kind? Will it make the situation better or worse?

- Be aware of how you feel physically. Is your heart racing? Is your face flushed? Is your breathing fast or hard? If the answer to any of these questions is yes, you may need to take a moment to meditate or practice a breathing exercise. It is important to remain calm in every situation, especially during tense or heated situations.

Here are a few strategies for managing your anger:

- First - acknowledge the issue.
- Second - keep a journal that details each angry experience you have. You will need to write down what happened, why it happened, and how you reacted to what it happened. It is so important to learn how to identify your triggers and acknowledge when you may have overreacted to something. This journal will help you learn more about yourself, and will help you learn to recognize your triggers before they have triggered you.
- Third - make sure you have a solid network of support. Consider sharing with your significant other, your family, or your closest friends that you are trying to learn how to manage your anger. Ask them to keep an extra eye out for you, to help you identify your triggers, and to help you calm down when your anger takes over. Not only can they motivate you, support you, and help you learn, but hearing you acknowledge your issues will strengthen your relationship with them.
- Fourth - when your emotions get away from you, and

you find yourself overwhelmed with anger, use an "interruption technique." These techniques are meant to literally interrupt your reaction and give you the opportunity to take a step back and regain control of yourself. Interruption techniques include:

- ○ Practicing a deep breathing exercise.
- ○ Counting to twenty.
- ○ Meditating for ten minutes.
- ○ Taking a short walk around the neighborhood.
- ○ Journaling about what has upset you.
- ○ Listening to your favorite song.
- ○ Reminding yourself of all the good things in your life.

- Fifth - practice empathy. If someone has made you angry, make a point to imagine yourself in their shoes and try to understand why they did what they did or said what they said. This will help you realize that they may not have intended to anger you, and will help you remember that they are people too, and are deserving of your empathy and understanding.
- Sixth - find a way to laugh at yourself. Step back and listen to what you say when you are angry. Odds are that what you say is pretty ridiculous and over-the-top. You may even want to ask your spouse to write down some of your outbursts so that you can revisit them later when you are clear-headed. This will help you recognize how prone you are to overreacting, and why people may respond to your anger by becoming disrespectful or even laughing at you.
- Seventh - learn to relax. Make a point to get plenty of sleep, eat a healthy diet, and exercise regularly. On top of that, consider practicing meditation or yoga on a daily

basis. Being mindful of your own needs, and acting on those needs, is crucial to finding a way to relax and deal with anger.

One of the great things about mindfulness meditation is that, once you get the hang of it, it can be practiced by anyone, just about anywhere and at any time. For starters, however, you are going to want to set aside about 15 minutes where you can find a quiet place to sit without having to worry about anyone bothering you. Once you are sitting in a relaxed position, all you need to do in order to get started is take several slow, deep, breaths. As you do so, focus on drawing as much sensory information from those breaths as possible. Consider the smells, the way the air feels as it feels your lungs and the way it tastes as it moves across your tongue.

From there you are going to want to expand you attention to include all of the other sensory information that your body is providing you with. The purpose of this is to help you to quiet the constant wave of thoughts that is likely moving through your mind. If you can quiet those thoughts, then it becomes easier to focus on the moment and leave your thoughts behind, at least for a little while.

While you remain in this meditative state, it is likely that you will still have thoughts that try and break through your reverie from time to time. When this occurs, it is important to not engage with the thought, or feel regret or anger that it has breached your defenses; instead all you need to do is picture the thought as if it were in a bubble and then simply let it float away. With practice, you will be able to access this type of mindset when you are dealing with more stressful issues, in order to help yourself remove negative thoughts from the conversation and focus on the situation.

- Eighth - remember to trust the people in your life. Angry individuals are often cynical as well, and they struggle to trust others. But honestly, if the people in your life have stuck around despite your anger issues, then they are probably worth trusting.
- Ninth - become an active listener. When you get angry, you only hear what you want to hear. You have to force yourself to stop and really listen to the person speaking to you. Remember to repeat what they have said back to them so that they have no doubt whether or not you heard what they had to say. You have to be engaged in the conversation, and not spend the entire time fuming and trying to formulate a response. Just listen!
- Tenth - be assertive, but not aggressive. An aggressive person is like a bulldozer, pushing their opinion and feelings at other people. An assertive person can express themselves clearly, but respectfully.
- Finally - remember how to forgive and forget. Holding grudges is not conducive to managing your anger. Grudges allow your anger to fester and boil under the surface, and you will inevitably drive people away as they will learn to fear having past mistakes thrown in their faces time and time again. You have to learn to forgive mistakes: consciously let them go, and then move on. Forgiving and forgetting is the most important tool you can have when it comes to managing your anger.

These tools will give you a great foundation and help you to master and manage your anger. Practice them daily!

Chapter 3: Taking Responsibility for Your Anger

As discussed earlier, the only person responsible for the way you feel is you. It is not the behavior of others that causes your irritation, frustration, or anger, it is the way you respond. If you can take responsibility for the way you respond, you can easily manage your anger.

If something is upsetting you, it is important to consider why it is upsetting you, and then extend that to why that person might be behaving or reacting in such an upsetting manner. Compassion and empathy are two of the most useful tools you have. If you can find a way to understand why someone is lying or acting in an unkind manner, it will be that much easier to forgive the behavior and move on. Letting bygones be bygones is a better choice, as opposed to allowing another person's behavior to anger you and have a negative effect on your life.

It is also important to remember that understanding anger does not mean it can be used as an excuse. You may understand why someone lied, but that does not mean you are overlooking the lie. And you can respond to a situation like that not with anger, but with understanding. Again, it does not mean you are overlooking or dismissing the lie.

Ultimately, you have to ask yourself this simple question: "Is my anger worth the damage it will cause to my life, my health, and my well-being?" The answer is always, always no. Your anger is never worth that.

Taking responsibility for your own anger also means that you should never take responsibility for the anger of others. Their anger is not your fault any more than your anger is their fault. If something happens, and a friend, coworker or spouse responds to you with anger, it is important to remind yourself that they are reacting that way because they have been conditioned to react that way. Their brains do not yet know how to respond differently.

If the people in your life struggle with anger in the same way that you do, you may want to consider teaming up and helping one another overcome the conditioned behaviors that are ruining your lives, health, and your well-being.

It never hurts to have someone by your side, someone who can support you when your emotions overwhelm you. Someone who can remind you when you are overreacting. Someone who can gently encourage you to meditate. And you can do the same for them.

If a particular event has upset you, use the following journal prompts to write about that event, and help you reflect on it with another person:

- What event happened?
- Did it cause pain or stress, and why?
- What were you thinking during those moments?
- On a scale of 0-10, how angry were you at that moment?
- On a scale of 0-10, how angry are you now?
- Did your behavior change as a result of your anger?
- Did the behavior of others change as a result of your anger?
- Before this happened, how did you feel? Were you already tense, stressed, irritated, and tired?
- How did your body respond to the situation? Did your heart start racing, did your palms start to sweat, or did

you get a headache?
- What did you want to do in that moment?
- Did you actually do what you wanted to do, or did you do something else?
- How do you feel about the situation now?
- Were there any consequences after the incident?

Grading Your Anger

You may find it helpful to gauge the level of your anger with the use of a simple grading scale. This can help you quantify your feelings and will help you discover the appropriate response for each situation.

For example, this is the grading scale that I use personally:

- A - I am not angry
- B - I feel irritation, but not anger
- C - I am angry
- D - I am angry, and I cannot control it
- F - I am so angry that I cannot function normally or behave in a kind or mature manner

When I write in my anger journal, I include my 'anger grade' at the top of each page. I like to revisit what I have written after I have calmed down, and tracking my 'anger grade' has been incredibly helpful in making sure that I am managing my anger correctly, recognizing my anger early, and responding to my anger effectively and maturely.

In addition, it is important to make healthy choices for yourself, especially if you are trying to manage your anger. Lack of sleep, a poor diet, and other unhealthy choices can exacerbate anger and make it difficult to manage.

You can improve your sleep habits in the following ways:

- **Getting 7 to 8 hours of sleep each night**
  After all, everyone is irritable when they are tired.

- **Limit caffeine and alcohol**
  This will help you fall asleep faster, and sleep more soundly.

- **Try not to nap during the day**
  As nice as a nap seems on the surface, it can actually disrupt your internal clock and confuse your brain.

- **Stop smoking**
  Nicotine is a stimulant, and like any stimulant, it can make it difficult for you to fall asleep and stay asleep.

- **Make sure your bedroom is a place of peace**
  Choose calming colors, keep the temperature cool, and make sure that the room is quiet. Listening to music or watching television to fall asleep can help too. Just make sure you use the 'sleep timer' feature when watching TV. This will help ensure that you are not subconsciously listening to the noise of the TV while you are sleeping to help improve the quality of your sleep.

Eating well and keeping healthy eating habits are highly recommended. Here are some basic tips:

- **Do not skip meals**
  No matter how busy you are, it is important to stop and eat. Your body cannot function properly without fuel. Skipping meals can make you irritable, or as some people call it: 'hangry.' If you tend to get hangry as a

result of a busy schedule or fast metabolism, consider keeping a small stash of healthy snacks in your desk, in your car, or in your purse. This will help soothe your hunger and the 'hangry' attitude until you can sit down and have a proper meal. Try not to rely on candy as your snack; try something a little more nutrient-dense, like granola bars, a piece of fruit, or a handful of nuts.

Chapter 4: Managing Your Anger

Anger manifests in many different ways and forms. Not everyone reacts the same way when they get angry. Some people yell, some people throw things, some people quietly seethe. It is different for everyone. This chapter will discuss each manifestation of anger to help you understand which of them matches yours. Once you understand your anger style, you can learn how to change your unhealthy behaviors and respond differently in the future.

A large number of people go around feeling at least a little angry all the time these days, and some have more justified reasons for this than others. Let's look at the differences between unjustified and justified anger.

Justified Anger

People who are justified in their anger are those who are hungry, who are taking on unmanageable tax burdens, who cannot afford housing or health care. Those who have lost loved ones to war or who don't feel as though they have a choice in political situations all have justified anger. Other situations where anger is justified might be homelessness, or inability to find employment or means for education, as well.

Unjustified Anger

Anger that stems from misplaced frustration or blame would be unjustified and unreasonable. The people who have unjustified anger include people who don't take responsibility for their own actions, who blame others for things beyond anyone's control, or who feel as though they are always being victimized by life circumstances. These are the people who always put their own needs first, and don't think about others.

Does Anger Give You the Illusion of Control?

If engaging in anger makes you feel as though you're actually in control, you will have a hard time ever controlling your anger. This heading sums up a lot of people's central problem with anger. For those who are interested in studying this emotion, it can be hard to find clinical literature on it. But this is starting to change. With drive-by shootings, road rage, and high school killing sprees on the rise, people are starting to play closer attention to those who are acting out, their extreme anger, and acts of aggression.

Suddenly, paying attention to warning signs of anger seems a lot more important. Within the last 15 years, at least 50 books have emerged on the subject of anger. In the year 1995, a professional book called *Anger Disorders: Definition, Diagnosis, and Treatment* came out that proposed some diagnostic categories to help professionals handle anger as its own syndrome, instead of connecting anger to various other disorders.

The following will help you make sense of the anger-related, self-defeating actions that arise from this emotion.

The Forgotten Defense

Anger can be thought of as the forgotten defense of Freud. If, in Freud's opinion, every defense mechanism of the human mind is there to protect our personalities from the effects of the ego being attacked, it seems unusual that he didn't consider anger as part of this process.

Anger as Camouflage

When it comes to an essential human feeling that is mainly there to protect someone from another feeling, anger might be the exception. Anger almost never exists as the main, primary emotion. Even when it appears to be a knee-jerk, instantaneous response to being provoked, there is usually another feeling that was there first. This primary feeling is what your anger is popping up to control or attempt to camouflage.

The Road Rage Example

A simple example of this idea of anger would be the extremely frustrating experience of someone cutting you off in traffic. Nearly everyone that experiences this event reacts with anger. However, when you look deeper at what getting cut off in traffic usually involves- the danger of getting into a life-threatening accident - you notice that at the moment before taking action to avoid the crash, you felt some kind of fear or apprehension.

Switching from this level of apprehension or fear to the intense state of anger occurs so quickly that most people can't recall the flash of fear they had felt before the anger or rage took over their mind. Rage itself appears to be a more desperate, stronger type of anger that was created in the mind to get rid of the threat to one's personal safety or ego, whether this is physical, emotional, or mental.

Secondary Anger and What It Means

The inner process happening in the above example also applies to other emotions that, once they appear, can be hidden through a flash of secondary anger. And as many psychological defenses get in the way of healthy coping mechanisms (by hiding the initial anxiety that must be faced), anger also shows how fragile the ego is that needs to be supported and shielded.

How Anger Controls Us

If anger leads us to a feeling of power and appears to be a magical solution to mask our deep fears and doubts, it's no wonder that it controls us in so many ways. In a way, anger is similar to cocaine, causing strong addictions due to its illusory effect of empowering us. Though almost no one realizes that their tendency toward getting angry is a way to cope with, intimidate, and disarm their enemy; anger is used as a way to make up for lack of self-esteem and personal power.

Unlike feeling out of control or weak, the emotion of aggression or anger can cause a sensation of invincibility or invulnerability. In fact, anger can even have physical effects on someone, making them momentarily stronger with adrenaline.

Anger for Distancing in Relationships

Anger also has a function in regulating the distance between us and others in close relationships, ensuring safety from getting hurt. If someone's parents or caretakers were untrustworthy, unreliable, or unresponsive, that person would probably grow up to be wary or defensive. They would likely cultivate a way to be emotionally detached in their relationships. Although these people might wish to form a strong bond that they've missed from childhood, they wouldn't know how to express these desires and needs in an open, healthy way. Risking this with someone who may react in a negative way could hurt them gravely.

The Fear of Letting down your Guard

The deep fear in these people is that letting their defense down and allowing themselves to be vulnerable, revealing their deep desire, could lead to rejection. A negative response could be very harmful to them, so they use anger as a protective measure and distance themselves as a way to survive emotionally.

Many spouses say that as soon as they notice their marriage going very well, their partner would pick a fight, probably due to feeling threatened by this closeness. Wounded psychologically from parental disregard, insensitivity, or even worse, they might have a serious distrust of getting too close to someone, defaulting instead to defensive anger as a way to protect themselves.

Using Anger to Push Someone Away

On the other hand, anger can also push others away from us, leading them to be the one to back away from the relationship first. If someone wants to get plenty of space and alone time, all he or she has to do is be angry all the time. This will cause others to avoid you at all costs. If you have no experience with relational intimacy, the feeling of being close to someone else can feel dangerous to your inner equilibrium, which sets off internal alarms, causing anger. In this sense, the anger can be said to be justified, but still not healthy to act upon.

Too much Detachment

But feeling very detached from others may also dredge up old fears and wounds, so sometimes, the one who wanted distance might pursue the other. What we can learn from this is that even unconscious anger can be used in many ways that regulate the feeling of vulnerability when it comes to close relationships. This can not only be utilized to create distance with the other person when closeness causes anxiety, but it can also be used as a way to try to engage the other person from a distance.

If a person had an insecure or tenuous attachment to his parents growing up, it's logical that the least risky way to get attached to someone else would be using anger to create distance. Scared of being too close to someone else, but scared of completely breaking our attachment to them, getting angry easily presents a solution, even though it's unsatisfying and dysfunctional. You can ask yourself the following questions to have a better understanding of your anger:

- What skills should I learn for controlling my anger?
- What is my anger supposedly protecting me against?
- How can I address the core feeling behind my anger?

Anger can be compared to an emotion that is just the tip of the iceberg. It's rarely there on its own, and instead exists to hide other, deeper emotions happening below it.

Explosive anger

This form of anger is exactly as it sounds, explosive. People who experience explosive anger often let their anger bubble under the surface for a long time, until the anger simply overloads their system and they explode as a result. This type of anger can be especially scary for the people around you when you release your anger all at once. People who do not know you well may think that your explosions of anger are sudden, unexpected, and extreme, but the people closest to you will likely recognize that the explosion is simply the result of a lot of buried anger. In fact, you are probably not even very angry about whatever it is that made you explode, you are probably holding on to anger about something that happened days or weeks earlier.

Have you ever found yourself screaming about something that is actually quite petty? Do you say things like, "If you leave your dirty towel on the bathroom floor one more time, I'm leaving you!" Are you actually mad about the towel? Probably not, as frustrating as that towel might seem. You are probably angry because you feel like your spouse or child does not help around the house as often as they should, or you are angry because you feel you have been disrespected by their lack of cleanliness. You are not actually furious about the single act of a towel being left on the floor.

So, what do you do to avoid explosions of anger?

Studies show that angry outbursts actually only last two or three seconds. Instead of letting your words escape from your mouth, count to ten. By the time you have counted to ten, odds are that you are calm enough to rethink what you were about to say. Simply rephrasing your angry statement can completely change the outcome of the conflict.

Instead of saying, "If you leave your dirty towel on the bathroom floor one more time, I'm leaving you," try something a bit more gentle, like, "It would mean a lot to me if you could be more aware of the mess you make."

Self-Abuse

This kind of anger involves blaming yourself for whatever has caused the conflict. Using the same example as before, consider how you would react if your spouse left their towel on the floor. Would you blame yourself? Would you decide that the reason they left it on the floor was because of you?

Your anger is your fault, but the stimulating event that caused your anger is not your fault. Why do you think it is your fault? It is important to really consider this question and discover why you feel that way. You may need to work on your own self-esteem, and your feelings of self-worth. The actions of someone else are never your fault.

Avoidance

With this form of anger, you will likely to translate your anger into other habits to pretend you are not angry or pretend that everything is okay and you have nothing to be angry about. This behavior usually manifests with self-destructive behavior like overeating, excessive spending, drug or alcohol use, and sleeping a lot.

People who express anger in this way likely came from households where other family members expressed anger in violent or volatile ways, so they learn to bury and hide their own anger, rather than dealing with their anger properly.

Avoiding the problem is never wise: you will eventually reach the point where the situation is totally and completely unmanageable, and you have absolutely no control over your reaction or the reactions of those around you. The situation may even reach a point where the consequences are irreparable.

If your avoidance tactic is to overeat, and you do not make an effort to control the situation or your reaction to it, you will eventually find yourself in an incredibly unhealthy place, both physically and emotionally. Constantly avoiding the problems in your life by overeating will only lead to obesity, diabetes, high blood pressure, and other serious, life-threatening health issues.

You have to learn to recognize when you are avoiding your anger and find a way to express your anger before it becomes excessive. Doing so could save your life!

Sarcasm

This form of anger can be particularly damaging to your interpersonal relationships. It may feel good in the heat of the moment to make a sharp, cutting remark about what has upset you, but that response is unfair, mean, and unhealthy.

Consider how it feels when the roles are reversed. Does it feel good when someone directs a cutting, sarcastic remark towards you? It does not. Rude remarks only serve to damage the self-esteem and self-worth of those involved, and can create distrust and negativity between two people.

No matter how angry you are, no matter why you are angry, no matter what about, it is important to always, always respond with kindness. Without kindness, relationships cannot survive, whether they are friendships, romantic relationships, or familial relationships.

Passive Aggressive

This form of anger is much like the act of 'avoidance' you previously read about. Instead of expressing your anger in a healthy way, you might choose to act in a vindictive manner by deliberately finding ways to make the lives of others more difficult, especially if the person in question was involved in whatever has upset you.

If you are angry about something at work, you may find yourself reacting in petty ways, such as using the last of the copy paper in the office printer. Instead of refilling the machine with paper before you leave, you walk away and let the next person deal with it, hoping it causes them irritation. No matter what you are upset about, reacting in this manner is immature, inappropriate, and petty.

Another example: Your boss asks you to stay late for a staff meeting and does not care that you have already had plans that evening. Instead of handling the issue maturely, you decide to show up to the meeting late. It might make you feel better in the moment, but your actions likely mean that the meeting runs even longer than anticipated, and that affects every single person at the meeting, including you. Your anger has then affected a lot of people that you had no reason to be angry with.

Habitual Irritation

This kind of anger usually manifests in a lot of tiny moments that seem innocuous but are actually having a very negative effect on your interpersonal relationships. Habitual irritation refers to being 'bothered by' tiny tasks that do not really matter.

Do you have a coworker who always wants to borrow your stapler? Do you find that irritating? Consider the moment. Are you actually upset because he or she wants to borrow your stapler, or are you upset about something a bit bigger? Perhaps it is because your coworker is disorganized or unprepared, and you feel they should have learned better by now? Odds are, the stapler is not what is really bothering you.

If this is the kind of anger that you have, it is important for you to really think about what is actually upsetting you and how your frustrated outbursts might be affecting your relationships. If you snap at someone every time they ask to use your stapler, they will eventually stop asking if they can use it and might tell other colleagues that you are unhelpful. Not because they understand why you are upset, but because they are afraid of your reaction, and afraid of being the target of your outburst.

Now that you understand the different ways anger can present itself, have you discovered what type of anger you typically experience and act upon? Understanding your particular brand of anger will help you identify that anger before you experience it, and this will help you learn how to control your anger and handle your reactions in a healthier manner.

As previously discussed, anger is a perfectly natural response to what you may unconsciously perceive as a threat. The first step in managing your anger is managing your response to anger. You can do this by identifying what makes you angry, as well as identifying the first emotional and physical signs of your anger. Learn how to step away from situations that are likely to anger you, and learn how to calm yourself down when those situations simply cannot be avoided.

Teach yourself not to dwell. Constantly revisiting whatever made you mad will only make you angrier. It is an entirely unproductive and ineffective use of your time and energy. Focus instead on the positive qualities of the person who angered you, or the positive qualities of the situation you were faced with. There is always a silver lining - you just have to look for it.

Much of anger management is simply changing the way you think. This is far easier said than done, but it can be done! You can do this in the following ways:

- Remove "always" and "never" from your vocabulary. Using these words is an attempt to justify your anger, and they will only alienate the people you are directing them towards.
- Be logical. Justifiable anger can still become irrational or disproportionate anger. Try to remind yourself that the world is not centered on YOU. Try to maintain a balanced perspective.
- Rephrase your expectations as desires. Do not demand things of others, under any circumstance. This can come across as aggressive and negative. Instead of saying, "You have to do it this way," simply say, "I would prefer that you do it this way." By changing the way you phrase it, you remove the negative connotation connected to your statement. This will make other more likely to cooperate with you.

Another strategy for coping with your anger is to relax. Deep breathing exercises, visualizing relaxing imagery, listening to classical music or nature sounds, using aromatherapy like lavender or eucalyptus - these tools can help to minimize your angry emotions and allow you to better cope with whatever is happening to you. As silly as it may sound, counting to ten can be very beneficial, and is always an accessible tool.

You should also work on your communication skills. Angry situations typically lead to miscommunications and difficulty understanding one another. Anger causes people to jump to conclusions, to make assumptions, and to react without listening or thinking. If you need to step away from the situation and take a few moments to calm down, do so. Nothing can be resolved if the parties involved cannot speak to one another calmly and respectfully.

You should also practice regular physical exercise. This will help you decompress, burn off the stressful energy you feel, and relieve any underlying tension. Exercise is one of the most flexible tools for managing your anger: depending on the type of exercise you choose, it can give you the chance to be alone if you need it, or to socialize with others in a group activity if that is what you need instead.

But most importantly, you should learn to recognize and avoid your triggers. If you know that traffic makes you angry, change the route you take to work, or start taking the bus. If you get angry when you see how messy your child's room is, simply shut the door so that you no longer have to see the mess. Do not seek out what may make you angry.

Deep Breathing

Deep breathing exercises are highly recommended. These exercises allow you to take a series of slow, steady, and deep breaths for up to ten minutes. Breathe in for four long counts, and then breathe out for four long counts. Use your diaphragm muscle to control your breath: imagine that the breath is coming from your gut, as opposed to your chest. Deep, even breathing should help slow down your heart rate and reduce your blood pressure.

Relaxing Imagery

You have probably heard of "going to your happy place." If you could go on vacation anywhere in the world, where would you go? Once you have answered that question, hold onto your answer. Next time you get angry, imagine yourself on that vacation. Take a few moments to daydream about it. You may be surprised how much this can help.

Meditation & Yoga

Any non-strenuous physical activity, like yoga or meditation, can help you relax and find a renewed sense of peace. Consider joining a yoga class, and practicing once or twice a week. There are many meditation programs available for free, so sample what's out there and try one that sounds like you would find it relaxing. Start small, with a five- to ten-minute guided meditation for beginners; you will not be comfortable with a two-hour advanced meditation as your first attempt! The benefits of meditation may take a few sessions for you to notice, so don't give up.

Problem Solving

For every problem, there is a solution. This may sound like just another cliché, and it may not bring you much comfort in times of anxiety or crisis, but it is nonetheless true. Instead of focusing on your anger and letting it control the situation you are in, focus on finding a solution. Take it one step at a time, and try to do what you can (even if it is minimal) to resolve the situation. Do not punish yourself or beat yourself up for what has happened. Do not blame others or point the finger. Take a deep breath and map out a plan of action. Doing so will make you feel more in control, which will automatically reduce your anger.

Communicate

If something has made you angry, talk about it. Just be sure to talk about it in a calm and constructive way. Never allow yourself to become disrespectful or hurtful towards others. If you need to talk to someone outside of the situation first, do it. Find a friend or family member and take a moment to vent to them about whatever has made you angry. Once you've got that off your chest, consider discussing the issue with those directly involved. Again, your conversation needs to be calm, constructive, rational and respectful. Try not to get defensive or hyper-critical. Using "I" language is helpful, especially in talking about the hurt or fear you feel when certain things happen. Think before you speak, and remember to use kind language.

Laugh

They say laughter is the best medicine, and that can be true even when it comes to anger. Nothing can defuse an angry situation faster than honest laughter. If you cannot laugh at yourself, then take a moment to look for some silly or funny videos online; this may help you redirect your emotions and calm down. Whatever you do, though, do not allow your anger to become mean, petty or sarcastic. This could be more harmful than the anger.

Change the Environment

Remember to take a break when you need to. If something happens at work to anger you, ask your supervisor if you can take a break and then take a short walk outside of the building. Remove yourself from the situation, and you will find it easier to calm down. If something happens at home, and you cannot leave, tell everyone in the house to give you some space and then take a bath or even a short nap. Taking a few moments for yourself will better prepare you for the conflict that awaits when you return.

Counseling

If you think you need to seek counseling, do it. There is no shame in seeking therapy from a professional for anger management. In fact, there is no shame in doing anything to better your life! Most psychologists agree that, with regular therapy, it only takes two months for someone to make significant strides in managing their anger.

Chapter 5: Stop Anger Before It Starts

Discussed in the previous chapter are the different manifestations of anger, and how to recognize which is your typical response. Now that you have this information, let us begin discussing how to stop your anger before it gets worse, one step at a time.

Because this is a learned behavior, you will have to re-learn, or completely retrain your brain to respond differently. To do this, you have to unravel your current reaction. When you want to swap out the laces on your sneakers, you cannot start at the bottom of the laces, you have to start at the top and work your way down.

Does your anger stem from something you were taught as a child? The following is a list of 'lessons' that many children are taught which may have contributed to the anger issues you have today:

- Boys should not cry
- Feelings are less important than logic
- Keep your feelings to yourself
- If you respond with anger, you will get attention
- Negative attention is better than no attention
- The way other people feel is more important than the way you feel
- If it might make someone unhappy, you should not do it
- Follow the rules no matter how silly the rules are
- Do not argue

Many times, children are taught that their opinions have no value and that they should simply "do as they are told," all of the time. This does not encourage communication or the healthy expression of emotions, and for many people, these attitudes develop into anger issues which can leave them having difficulty communicating with others later on in life.

If you have children at home, you may want to look closely at the way you treat them and the things you say to them. While your children should absolutely respect your instructions, it is important to give them the opportunity to understand why you want them to do something 'your way.' It is important to give them the opportunity to express themselves in a safe place.

Remember, emotions are subjective. They are never wrong. They are often mismanaged and misunderstood, but they are never wrong. Every person of any age needs to know that their emotions are valid and important and worthy of understanding.

There are a number of different ways you can handle your anger. Here are just a few:

Relaxing

It may seem silly, but breathing exercises can be truly helpful. If you find that you have trouble getting through a breathing exercise on your own, consider searching for videos on YouTube that can help teach you the techniques. There are some videos that will help you complete a breathing exercise over five or ten minutes, and they may even provide relaxing music or imagery to accompany the exercise.

Part of many breathing exercises is breathing deeply. If you visualize pulling the breath from your diaphragm (or your gut), it can help you take a truly deep breath. Take several slow deep breaths over a short period of time, and you may notice that your heart rate will slow, your blood pressure will drop, your hands will be steady, and you will feel calmer overall.

Some people find that it is helpful to repeat certain phrases to themselves during the exercise like "Take it easy," "Breathe in, breathe out," or "Relax." Or they may find certain music that has a calming effect like classical compositions or even music from their favorite singer.

Relaxing imagery can be beneficial, too. Many people can easily visualize a 'happy place' or a paradise. Simply close your eyes, breathe deeply, and imagine that you are in your happy place, far away from whatever has upset you. Doing this can have an incredibly calming effect.

These tools are incredibly helpful in the heat of the moment, but it is also important to practice relaxing exercises on a daily or weekly basis. This will help reduce stress and prevent your anger from spiraling out of control.

Consider practicing yoga on a regular basis. Yoga will help you relieve tension, relax, and find peace. It is also a healthy practice, physically. Yoga will increase your flexibility and muscle tone, burn calories, and more.

If you practice these skills frequently, they will become second nature to you. You will find yourself automatically practicing your breathing exercises whenever you feel anger poisoning your mood.

Cognitive Reconstruction

The next step is to start changing the way you think. You may notice that when you are angry, you are more likely to swear, insult others, react dramatically, exaggerate, or behave irrationally.

If one thing goes wrong, do you respond by immediately believing everything will go wrong, forever? Instead, remind yourself that despite how you may feel, it is not the actual end of the world. Tell yourself something like this: "This is frustrating, but it is understandable. Getting angry about it now will not solve anything. And it is not the end of the world."

Avoid using words like "always," "never," and "forever." Avoid swearing or using negative language. Make an effort not to say something that might alienate, humiliate, or insult the person you are talking to. Anger has never fixed a problem, it has only delayed you from finding a solution.

Use logic to help yourself. Everyone has bad moments or bad days. Everyone experiences bad luck. It is important to remember that the universe does not hold a grudge against you, and it is not out to make you miserable. Look at this way, the universe has better things to worry about than messing things up for you.

Also, remember that you cannot let your anger make demands from other people. Everyone wants to be treated fairly, to be appreciated, and to have others agree with them. But these things are not guarantees. They are not owed to you. All these things come from respect, and respect has to be earned. You cannot demand respect if you are not prepared to give respect as well. Anger and respect cannot coexist.

Problem-solving

One of the most important things you should remember is that not every problem has a solution and not everything can be fixed. Instead of focusing on a solution, focus on how you are supposed to handle the problem. Keeping a positive attitude and making a serious attempt to approach the problem with a clear head, clear conscious, and sense of maturity, are the best things you can do for yourself.

Communicate

For a lot of people, anger stems from a lack of communication or an inability to communicate effectively or positively. It can not only cause anger, but it can also exacerbate anger. Anger leads to assumptions and inaccurate conclusions.

The first step to clearer communication is to not say the first thing that comes to mind. In a heated moment, you are likely to say something unkind or even cruel. Sometimes, the best response is simply not to respond.

The second step to clearer communication is to truly and actively listen. It is easy to bury yourself in your thoughts and feelings without ever truly considering the thoughts and feelings of the person you are in conflict with.

You should ask one another the following questions:

- How do you feel?
- Why do you feel that way?
- What can I do to make you feel differently?

If you can have an open and honest discussion with one

another and truly get to the root of the problem, then you can also work together to fix the issue. It is important to remember that the problem probably will not be solved overnight, and it may take a lot of time and a lot of hard work. But it can be solved if both parties can keep their anger and irrationality out of the equation.

For many people, the first response to conflict is to be defensive, especially when criticized by someone else. However, when a person allows himself to be defense, he will not hear the *real* problem is nor will he understand his role in the problem. This leaves the other person feeling neglected, ignored, unimportant, and sometimes invisible. No one should seek to make another person feel this way. Not a spouse, not a child, not a friend, and not even a stranger.

Humor

Another great way to handle anger is through humor. Light-heartedness will humanize the situation and bring everyone together as they laugh together. It will defuse the tension, give everyone a chance to breathe, and remind everyone involved that the situation is not entirely awful. There is a silver lining to everything, and that silver lining is often humor.

Environment

Another way to manage your anger is by changing your environment. Sometimes, taking a walk or a drive is a good way to defuse the tension you are experiencing, and provide a new perspective. It can be hard to remain calm and collected if you remain in an environment that is upsetting to you.

For example, if you come home from work to find that your children have left your house a mess, it may be best to calmly ask your children to tidy up and to then take a walk around the block to collect yourself before returning home. If you stay at home and watch as your children tidy up, you may find it harder to calm down. Standing over them as they clean, the only thing you will think about is the fact that they did not clean earlier or maybe that they are not cleaning correctly. Instead, take a walk. By the time you get home, hopefully, your children have done exactly as you calmly asked, and you will return to a relatively clean home.

Another thing that may help is preventing your environment from being interrupted. If you had a rough day at work, and just need a few minutes for yourself, do not be afraid to ask for those few minutes. When you get home, ask your family to give you some space. Take that time for yourself and do something that you really enjoy. Take a bath, read a book, or play a video game. Once your nerves have settled, rejoin your family and get back to your normal routine. Everyone will be thankful that you took the time to calm down, rather than letting something that happened outside of the home affect those inside of the home.

Making Changes

Are there certain things in your life that just always make you angry? Maybe your kids do not keep their rooms as clean as you would like. Maybe your commute to work is stressful. Make small changes that will allow you the chance to breathe.

If you get angry every time you walk past your child's dirty bedroom, simply shut the door. Have a calm and honest discussion with your child about why it is important to keep their room clean, but do not allow your child's behavior to have a negative effect on how you view your life. Shut the door to their bedroom so that you are not constantly reminded of how messy it is. Remove that trigger, and you are less likely to be angered by their disobedience. Children will respond more positively to a calm and rational parent than to one who is extremely angry over something they deem to be 'silly.'

Do you arrive at work angry because you had a long and stressful commute? Change the route on the way back! Pick a different busy street to drive down. The change in routine may be enough to shake you out of your irritation and provide a change of scenery that will help distract you from the traffic and stress, even if the level of traffic and stress are the same on your new route.

Chapter 6: Keeping Anger Out of Your Life

Now that you have learned how to identify what makes you angry, and you have learned how to manage that anger, it is time to closely examine the parts of your life that repeatedly bring anger and stress into your life.

Look closely at your relationships, your job, and your home life. Is there someone in your life that deliberately makes you angry? Someone that cannot manage their own anger? Someone who chooses to create conflict, drama, or tension in your home, your work, or your life?

If this person is unwilling or unable to work with you in managing your anger, your overall health, and well-being, and if this person does not want what is best for you, it may be time to consider removing them from your life. If you cannot completely avoid a person, you can keep them from talking to you by always having a reason to walk away.

Sometimes, the toxic relationship is with a significant other. Sometimes it is with a co-worker or boss. Sometimes it may even be with a family member or a friend. Everyone experiences a toxic relationship at one time or another. If you discover that you are in one, it is important not to blame yourself for it. You cannot choose how someone treats you, but you can choose how you react to the way you are treated.

Removing toxic relationships from your life is never easy. It can be incredibly hard to admit that you were wrong about someone, or that they do not have your best interests at heart. But removing toxic relationships from your life is not only necessary for managing your anger, but it is also necessary for you to achieve happiness. It is necessary for maintaining a healthy, happy, and fulfilling life.

You may find yourself walking away from your spouse or significant other. You may find yourself disowning some family members. You may even find yourself quitting your job or asking to be transferred out of the toxic environment you have found yourself in.

The important thing that you will always want to remember is that the toxic relationship is not your fault, which means you don't need to fix it (or the person) by yourself. Staying away from them is the only responsibility you have. You are not responsible for or at fault for the actions of others, just as no one else is responsible for or at fault for your actions. You are your own person, and that cannot be ignored or denied.

It has been suggested that you must have a journal. There you can write what makes you angry and why. Now, start a second journal. There, write what makes you happy or brings you joy and why. These prompts will serve as a reminder that even though your life is not perfect, there is an awful lot of good in it.

Conclusion

Managing your anger is not meant to be easy. It requires a wealth of commitment, introspection, and a lot of hard work. It will not happen overnight, or even over the next week. It will take months of hard work to get a handle on your anger, and then it will take years of consistent commitment to maintain that handle on your anger.

Managing your anger is a process. It will help you identify what triggers you have, and it will help you handle tense or stressful situation in a healthy and constructive manner. The purpose of anger management is not to avoid all anger, but to minimize it. The purpose of anger management is to limit the amount of physical or emotional stress you experience on a daily basis. Hopefully this book has helped you learn how to control the way you react in moments of anger. If you find that the tools within this book are not enough to help you manage your anger, then you may need to seek the help of a mental health professional or anger management counselor. Everyone experiences anger, and for some people, that anger can be overwhelming, so do not feel ashamed if you want additional help.

Remember:

- Keep a journal to help you identify your triggers, and to better understand your overreactions.
- Become an active listener and learn to focus on what others are saying to you, instead of focusing on how you want to respond.

- Practice your interruption techniques when your anger becomes more than you can handle. Meditate, take a walk, and listen to your favorite song. Remember to take a moment to collect yourself. Not every situation or conversation requires an immediate response from you, and there is absolutely nothing wrong with asking for a moment to breathe.

You cannot avoid anger in life, but you can manage it, and you can stop it from controlling your life, ruining your relationships, or damaging your career. Remember: anger is ultimately your responsibility. You cannot blame others for the way you choose to react, now that you know better.

May this book have helped you manage your anger much easier. By applying the methods provided in this book, you will find yourself becoming happier, healthier, and calmer.

Finally, if you found this book useful in any way, a review on Amazon is always appreciated!